Christ and Calamity

*Grace & Gratitude
in the Darkest Valley*

HAROLD L. SENKBEIL

LEXHAM PRESS

Christ and Calamity: Grace and Gratitude in the Darkest Valley

Copyright 2020 Lexham Press

Lexham Press, 1313 Commercial St., Bellingham, WA 98225
LexhamPress.com

"Prayer in Time of Affliction" adapted from *Collects and Prayers for
Use in the Church* (Philadelphia: The United Lutheran Church in
America, 1935), p. 115.

Artwork on pages i, xiii, 127, 128, 132, 138, and 147 is copyright 2019
Jonathan Mayer (www.ScapegoatStudio.com). Used by permission.
All rights reserved.

Unless otherwise noted, all Scripture quotations are from the
ESV® Bible (*The Holy Bible, English Standard Version®*), copyright
© 2001 by Crossway Bibles, a publishing ministry of Good News
Publishers. Used by permission. All rights reserved.
The quotation on p. 30 is the ESV alternate translation; the
quotation on p. 40 is adapted from the ESV.

Scripture quotations marked (KJV) are from the King James
Version. Public domain.

Hardcover Print ISBN 9781683594451
Digital ISBN 9781683594444
Library of Congress Control Number 2020939428

Lexham Editorial: Todd Hains, Abigail Stocker, Danielle Thevenaz
Cover Design: Brittany Schrock
Book Design and Typesetting: Abigail Stocker

Jesus,
I am yours; save me.

PSALM 119:94

In Thine arms I rest me;
Foes who would molest me
Cannot reach me here.
Though the earth be shaking,
Ev'ry heart be quaking,
Jesus calms my fear.
Lightnings flash
And thunders crash;
Yet, though sin and hell assail me,
Jesus will not fail me.

Contents

Invitation to the Reader

Christ and calamity go together. As Jesus said: "In the world you will have tribulation. But take heart; I have overcome the world" (John 16:33). When calamity strikes, you need Jesus.

This little book is filled with Jesus. Here you will find him quoted frequently, as well as many other Bible passages, all to help you through the rough spots in life.

Tackle this book prayerfully.

God's word and prayer are the means by which he sanctifies all things—even tribulation and distress. And so I have included prayers of consolation that pair well with the themes in this book. You will find a prayer at the beginning of this book and then three sets of prayers—for any time, for morning, and for evening—and a hymn at the end.

You can use this material on your own or with others. The material at the end would work especially well in a group setting—it's arranged as responsive prayer, with one person speaking and the rest answering with the words in bold.

In the dark valleys of life you don't need platitudes. You need Jesus. Read this book with open ears and an open heart, and you will find consolation, solace, and peace in him.

In times of calamity we need the unvarnished truth. Tribulation will occur in this world. Jesus said so. But it's also true that he has overcome the world.

And in his cross and resurrection there's hope for you.

Harold L. Senkbeil
Pentecost 2020

Prayer in Time of Affliction

Call upon me in the day of trouble;
I will deliver you, and you shall glorify me.

PSALM 50:15

LORD, you know the deep places through which our lives must go: Help us, when we enter them, to lift our hearts to you; help us to be patient when we are afflicted, to be humble when we are in distress; and grant that the hope of your mercy may never fail us, and the consciousness of your lovingkindness may never be clouded or hidden from our eyes; through Jesus Christ, your Son, our Lord. *Amen.*

Your Calamity

I write these opening lines on a stunningly gorgeous day—one of the first we've had here in Wisconsin during the lingering winterish springtime that has added insult to the injury of our months-long stay-at-home lockdown. Neighbors are out doing early yard work; tulips and daffodils wave in the sunshine; robins splash in my birdbath.

Yet something isn't quite right.

More people than usual are walking by with their dogs on a leash or their children in tow. They smile and wave at me, but they are wary of each other. Joggers head into the street to avoid closely approaching the other humans on the sidewalk. Many are masked in public to avoid spreading an unseen contagion.

Few cars drive by my house today. The price of crude oil went to negative digits not long ago—a decline accelerated by quarantines the world over. The stock market took a dive months ago and is making its first furtive efforts at recovery. Yet analysts warn that it will be a rocky road. Globally, markets lost more than 30 percent of their value. People are out of work in record numbers. Businesses are languishing because of precautionary shutdowns; many will never reopen.

We are facing a worldwide pandemic of infectious disease caused by a new virus the likes of which we have never before seen during our lifetimes. Millions of people have contracted the disease. Some have grown gravely ill, and hundreds of thousands have already died. Governments all over the world have responded by restricting our travel and imposing quarantines to limit human contact and slow the contagion. Alarming rumors swirl. Media have fanned the flames of public fear to near-panic proportions. Seemingly overnight, the world as we knew it was turned upside down. Daily life morphed into a surreal simulation of what it once was.

Now in our seventies, my wife and I are told we are especially vulnerable to this public health threat. Our grown children enforce their own private quarantine. They distance themselves to avoid inadvertently infecting us if they are symptomless carriers of the virus. It's hard. We're not an especially expressive family, but air hugs are no substitute for a real embrace. Grandma and Grandpa are going through withdrawal; we long for the day we can regularly put our arms around our grandchildren again.

Businesses, governmental agencies, and churches have embraced new technology and implemented digital connections to avoid flesh-and-blood interaction. A gradual reopening, predicted in the months ahead, will most likely happen in fits and starts. No one really expects "normal" to return anytime soon, if ever. It's as if someone pushed pause on our daily routine, and we're all marking time while infectious disease experts scramble to find effective means to treat the illness and epidemiologists look for ways to anticipate and stem the spread of infection that has disrupted our lives.

B ut this is not a book about the coronavirus or the COVID-19 pandemic. This is a book about you. Rather, it's about you and God—and how you relate to him in times of calamity. To be exact, this is a book about God's faithfulness in the face of uncertainty.

In the eleven short chapters of this book, I will talk with you about how you can count on God to keep his promises, even when you can't see him or feel him. How you can trust him even when it seems like he's untrustworthy. Even when you face an uncertain future. Even while you are doubting or when you are afraid.

It doesn't have to be a coronavirus that you're facing. It could be another illness. It could be excruciating and unrelenting pain. It could be overwhelming sadness or debilitating depression. It could be the breakup of your marriage or your household. It could be the loss of someone you love. It could be the loss of your health, or the impending loss of your own life.

This book is an invitation to hope—because ultimately, this is a book about faith. Let's talk for a moment about that: faith, of course, is foundational for Christians. But faith is not sight, and so, by definition, faith is not the same as knowing for certain. Scripture reminds us: "Hope that is seen is not hope. For who hopes for what he sees? But if we hope for what we do not see, we wait for it with patience" (Romans 8:24–25). Waiting patiently for something hoped for is a good working definition of faith, and that's what I want to talk to you about in these pages: trusting God for help when you can't detect any available remedy. I want to lend you courage and consolation in the face of whatever personal calamity you face.

Calamities come in different sizes. Sometimes they are comparatively minor—not much more than minor inconveniences, when you get right down to it. But other calamities are serious disruptions or overwhelming tragedies. But one thing about calamities, large or small: they get your attention. They lead you to think about God for a change. As C. S. Lewis wrote long ago: "Pain insists upon being attended to. God whispers to us in our pleasures, speaks in our consciences, but shouts in our pains. It is his megaphone to rouse a deaf world."[1]

Public responses to the current pandemic certainly have called our world out of its spiritual doldrums. But I have a hunch your personal calamities have a similar impact on you individually. God shouts at us in our private catastrophes, doesn't he? The question is, what is he saying? And more to the point, how will we respond?

Private or public calamity always calls for faith—confident trust in God, despite our apprehensions.

St. Matthew records that Jesus' disciples faced a test of their faith on the Sea of Galilee. As they ferried him across the lake, a violent storm came up, threatening to swamp their boat. They were amazed to discover their Lord fast asleep in the midst of the storm, so they shook him awake: "Save us, Lord; we are perishing."

That's a pretty normal reaction to impending disaster. We've all been there in the middle of our own private or public calamities—we cry out in fear, at least inwardly: "Lord, don't you care if we perish? How about helping us out? Save us!" Jesus did still the storm, rescuing the beleaguered boatmen, but not before he gently chided them: "Why are you afraid, O you of little faith?" (8:25).

A few chapters later, we read of a similar incident of peril on the sea. But this time, Peter is the one in trouble. In the middle of a stormy nighttime crossing the disciples were frightened when they spotted a ghostly figure walking toward their boat on the wind-tossed waves. But then they heard a familiar voice: "Take heart; it is I. Do not be afraid" (14:27). True to form, Peter impetuously challenged Jesus: "Lord, if it is you, command me to come to you on the water." Upon Christ's invitation, Peter took one step and then another on the waves, walking on the water. But when he saw the mighty wind, he began to sink and cried out in alarm for help. Jesus stretched out his hand and pulled him up, saying, "O you of little faith, why did you doubt?"

Peter doubted for the same reason you and I doubt when we're faced with uncertainty and calamity. We wonder what's to become of us. Sometimes our fear can be overwhelming. We're fearful in the face of tragedy and the unknown because we've never passed this way before; the terrain is unfamiliar, and the perils are formidable.

Fear is a perfectly normal response in these situations. And truth be told, our faith isn't as strong as it could be. Like the disciples in the middle of the storm and like Peter sinking in the waves, we are people of small faith.

But here's the thing about faith. What matters isn't the amount of faith we have; it's the object of our faith. The Lord in whom we trust is what matters. When we call out to him, even in fear or doubt, he's there to hear and to save— though it's true that his remedy may not match our expectations. Think of Peter, out on the waves:

Peter's faith may have been small, but he had a great and mighty Lord. His faith may have been weak, but the hand of Jesus was strong to save.

He will save you, too. No matter how small your faith, you can count on him to hear your anguished cry and answer in his own time and way.

If we have died with him,
we will also live with him;
if we endure,
we will also reign with him;
if we deny him,
he also will deny us;
if we are faithless,
he remains faithful—
for he cannot
deny himself.

2 Timothy 2:11–13

II

When You Are Faithless, Christ Is Your Faithfulness

F aith, as a subjective experience, is forever in flux. Sometimes it feels like "God's in his heaven; all's right with the world." Some Christians go on like this for days at a time, even weeks on end, with nary a twinge of uncertainty or doubt.

But that's not the norm. It's unrealistic to assume your faith should constantly seem strong and resilient; by its very nature, faith usually is mingled with doubt. That's because your faith differs from knowledge that you acquired by logical deduction. Though God indeed uses word and water, bread and wine to connect with us, ultimately faith itself is rooted not in tangible things but in invisible ones. It is "the assurance of things hoped for, the conviction of things not seen" (Hebrews 11:1).

For as long as we live, you and I will experience ups and downs in our life of faith. We can be at the top of our game at one moment and down in the depths in the next. Human emotions are like that, as you well know. Any number of things—what's going on in a given moment, even the phases of the moon or atmospheric conditions—can impact our mood.

Faith isn't an emotion. True, as we reflect on faith, it can often seem like a feeling. But faith is far more: Faith is the hand that grasps the promises of God. Faith is trust—faith is reliance on God and his word. It's a two-party arrangement, a mutual bond, and while God remains steady and firm, we often falter.

You can certainly see this dynamic playing out in the history of Israel and their faith. God chose their ancestral father Abraham, pledging to make of his descendants a great nation from which would come the redeemer he first promised in Eden. Through the centuries he repeatedly renewed his covenant relationship with them, promising to be their God over and over again. And in turn, generation after generation of Israelites promised to be his people.

Most strikingly of all, after their long bondage in Egypt, God delivered his people dramatically and miraculously from the swift chariots of Pharaoh's army at the Red Sea, leading them safely through the waters on dry ground and bringing them to the sacred mountain of Sinai. There, he personally appeared to Moses and the elders of Israel, renewing the covenant he first gave to Abraham and vowing once again to give them his gracious blessing and merciful hand to guide them. At Sinai God spoke to his people through his prophet Moses, giving them his law to bind them to himself. And with one voice the people of Israel responded: "All that the LORD has spoken we will do" (Exodus 19:8).

But what did the people *actually* do?

Even a casual review of the history of God's covenant people shows how fickle they were in their relationship with him. Repeatedly they turned to other gods instead of the Lord, who had brought them out of slavery in Egypt and delivered them with his mighty hand and outstretched arm. Repeatedly they broke his commands. Repeatedly they embraced the idolatrous, adulterous ways of the pagan nations among whom they lived.

You might think that their faithfulness would improve when God entered human history in person, born in human flesh. But no. The pattern of ancient Israel carries through in the church in the New Testament. While Jesus deliberately hand-picked his twelve disciples to found a new Israel, their faith faltered as well.

On the night in which he was betrayed, after the Last Supper, Jesus informed his disciples that they would all fall away when he was betrayed to his executioners. Peter objected: "Even if I must die with you, I will not deny you!" (Matthew 26:35). The other disciples said the same. Of course, before that night was over, Peter denied that he had ever known Jesus. The very next day at Golgotha, the whole crowd of disciples—with the exception of John, Jesus' mother, Mary Magdalene, and Mary of Cleopas—abandoned Jesus to die the agonizing, despicably shameful death of crucifixion.

I think I can understand Peter and his friends. At times, I'm utterly convinced that I can suffer anything—even death—and not depart from Jesus. At other times, I'm not so sure. Judging by my words and actions, the sad reality is that, like Peter, I repeatedly have denied the Lord who bought me with his blood. Over and over again I have failed to live according to the commandments of God's law. Not only have I done things God forbids, but just as grievously I have not done the things he commands.

I have lived as if God did not matter and as if I mattered most. My Lord's name I have not honored as I should; my worship and prayers have faltered. I have not let his love have its way with me, and so my love for others has failed. There are those whom I have hurt and those I have failed to help. My thoughts and desires have been soiled with sin.[2]

I suspect that it's much the same for you. But my point is not that you and I are sinners. Rather, I want to highlight what should be obvious but what we so often forget: our faith fluctuates from day to day. As a subjective, felt experience, it's on again, off again. Hot and cold, strong and weak, sturdy and frail.

B ut faith does not hinge on our feelings. It is rooted firmly in the promises of God. When "we are faithless, he remains faithful—for he cannot deny himself" (2 Timothy 2:13).

When calamity strikes, you can count on God— not because you feel close to him, but because he remains close to you, in his word, for Jesus' sake. In the midst of the uncertainties of your life you needn't wonder about his feelings or attitude toward you. Though your faith might fluctuate, his promises never waver: "all the promises of God find their Yes" in Christ Jesus (2 Corinthians 1:20).

In life's tight spots, focus not on your faith, but on God's faithfulness. Look not at your promises to him, but his loving promises to you in his Son. Rest assured, those promises include your name.

Then, freed from the continual teeter-totter of faith's emotional roller coaster, you can confidently utter your hearty "Amen" to God's eternal glory.

Before they call
I will answer;
while they are
yet speaking
I will hear.

Isaiah 65:24

III

When You Cry Out, Christ Is Your Advocate

H ave you ever noticed that when calamity strikes, after the initial shock wears off, our first thought is often, "Why me?" Somehow, we've gotten it into our heads that God's job is to make us happy and keep us happy. After all, he's God, isn't he? And doesn't God know everything? Doesn't he know that our present predicament isn't very pleasant?

Yes, he does. But what gave you the idea that the almighty Maker of heaven and earth is supposed to keep everything on an even keel? If you've read your Bible, you know that in the beginning, God created a good world; sin entered that world through one man, and death was the consequence. Now, like a deadly contagion, death has spread through all humankind, because all people sin (Romans 5:12).

God's pristine creation—with no suffering, no death, and no destruction—is now long gone. This earth is still a delightful place to live. But everywhere we look, our beautiful world is filled with misery, hardship, sickness, calamity—and death.

Though, by God's merciful grace, he works everything (even sorrow and pain) for the good of those who love him (Romans 8:28), the awful truth is that all misery comes from his gracious hand. God himself says so: "There is no god beside me; I kill and I make alive; I wound and I heal; and there is none that can deliver out of my hand" (Deuteronomy 32:39).

That sounds pretty harsh. I don't like it any more than you do. My wife and my best friend both live every day with chronic pain, the result of injuries and health conditions. I would do anything to even briefly relieve their suffering for just an instant. But I can't. And neither can you. That's our frustration: some things in this broken world simply can't be fixed, humanly speaking. It will do no good for us to whine about it. But there's something else I can recommend.

Instead of whining, try lamenting.

Have you noticed that in the Bible's hymnbook, the Psalms, roughly a third are songs of lament? You may know some of them by heart: "My God, my God, why have you forsaken me?" (Psalm 22). "Oh God, why do you cast us off forever?" (Psalm 74). "Why are you cast down, O my soul, and why are you in turmoil within me?" (Psalm 42). "Vindicate me, O God, and defend my cause against an ungodly people" (Psalm 43).

These psalms of lament teach us how to file a complaint with God. And complaining isn't whining; if you've ever read your medical records, you'll know that medical complaints are simply the physical symptoms of your distress. When you go to your doctor, you're not whining; you're just explaining where you hurt. You list your complaints because you know your condition should receive attention. It may not go away; some of the symptoms may remain. But you've gone to someone who can do something about it.

Likewise, lamenting is calling God's attention to what he already knows: you're hurting, and it's no fun. That miserable situation forces you to acknowledge that you aren't a self-made person. You depend on God for your very life—but sometimes it takes a fearsome calamity to impress that dependence upon you and bring you to the point of lament. That lament is a cry of faith.

And so God in his grace invites you to complain—to bring your hurts and your miseries to him. It's okay that these things feel too big for you; there's no real way to cope with disaster and tragedy on your own. It's important to not keep these troubles bottled up inside ourselves. Like any loving father, God, in his mercy, invites us to come to him and talk. So like little children, we crawl into his lap by means of our lament, telling him exactly where it hurts and asking him for help: "Turn, O LORD, deliver my life; save me for the sake of your steadfast love" (Psalm 6:4).

That's the hard part, isn't it: believing our God is gracious, even when tragedy strikes. We reason that if God is almighty, we shouldn't be in this predicament in the first place. By all appearances he either is unable to help or doesn't care.

That's why it's essential at all times—but especially in the midst of tragedy—that we rely not on our own speculations but rather on God's sure word. If we only draw on our experience of calamity, the steadfast love of the Lord will remain invisible. Looking at our pain and misery alone, we're tempted to conclude that God is angry with us.

But God's true perspective on human suffering is revealed not in our experience but in that of Jesus on the cross. There, God's own beloved Son suffered in great agony of body, mind, and spirit as the sinless victim of our sin, in order that he might bring us to God (1 Peter 3:18). Crucifixion was a bloody, gory, anguishing mess. In the midst of his deep physical and spiritual agony, Jesus too felt that God was against him. From the cross, he cried out: "My God, my God, why have you forsaken me?" (Matthew 27:46).

In times of calamity, we have hope: Christ himself is with us in our misery, and his suffering sanctifies our pain. Because he was abandoned, we will never be. Because of Jesus, our Father in heaven wraps us in his embrace. Before it was finished on that dark Friday, before Jesus breathed his last, he committed his spirit into the hands of his loving Father in fervent faith (Luke 23:46).

Because of Jesus, you can be certain that you have a loving Father to whom you can turn to list your complaints and misery—just as he did on his cross. Even though you see no available remedy, you are not shouting into an empty void when you pray. Though you are in distress, you can place yourself—your body and soul and all things—into his care, believing that for Jesus' sake, your Father in heaven fervently loves you and will see you through your present suffering.

Lamenting your hurt but trusting his cross-shaped love, you can confidently ask him to sustain you through all your days in faith-filled hope:

Return, O LORD! How long?
    Have pity on your servants!
Satisfy us in the morning with your steadfast love,
    that we may rejoice and be glad all our days.
Make us glad for as many days as you have
      afflicted us,
    and for as many years as we have seen evil.
Let your work be shown to your servants,
    and your glorious power to their children.
Let the favor of the Lord our God be upon us,
    and establish the work of our hands upon us;
    yes, establish the work of our hands!
                  (Psalm 90:13–16)

As the sufferings of
Christ abound for us,
so also our comfort
abounds through
Christ.

2 CORINTHIANS 1:5

IV

When You Are Afflicted, Christ Is Your Comfort

You may remember the bracelets that many Christians used to wear, which read WWJD: "What would Jesus do?" It's a good question. Actually, it's not a bad way to guide our decision-making. The world would be a better place if Christians showed Jesus' love and care in more of our interactions. And it would make a big difference if we reflected on that question before spouting off to our neighbors or unloading on our spouse, to cite just two common situations. WWJD, indeed.

Yet the question "what would Jesus do?" also oversimplifies the biblical record about Jesus' actions. Jesus responded differently in different situations. He cracked the whip at the money changers in the temple (John 2:15), yet he rebuked

Peter for his violence in Gethsemane (Matthew 26:52). Jesus praised the woman who extravagantly poured ointment over his head in Bethany (Matthew 26:6–13), yet he also commended the poor widow for her paltry offering (Luke 21:1–4). Jesus saw into the human heart in a way that we cannot, so it's hard for us to figure out what he would do in every situation.

But one WWJD always applies.

What would Jesus do? He would suffer. When you suffer as a Christian, you can know for certain that you're doing what Jesus would. It's what Jesus actually did! He didn't seek suffering, like some sort of cosmic masochist; rather, he suffered because he wanted us. He came to seek and save the lost, laying down his life as the ransom to free all humankind from bondage to sin, death, and hell.

His seeking and saving cost him dearly. Roman crucifixion was anything but tidy. This deliberately barbarous practice was implemented to keep Rome's captive people in submission. No Roman citizen could lawfully be put to death so cruelly. As in the case of Jesus, crucifixion usually involved being stripped and then mercilessly whipped before being nailed up to die a lingering, torturous death in naked, public shame. After days of starvation and exposure, most victims eventually died of asphyxiation—they could no longer raise themselves against the nails tearing at their flesh to gulp sufficient air to breathe.

It was an awful death for Jesus to die, yet all the blood and the gore of the cross was only the tip of the iceberg. The nineteenth-century hymnist Thomas Kelly put it well:

> Many hands were raised to wound Him,
> None would intervene to save;
> But the deepest stroke that pierced Him
> Was the stroke that justice gave.[3]

With his holy, precious blood and with his innocent suffering and death, Jesus faced God's wrath against us all. He was the Lamb of God, who takes away the sin of the world. At the cross, the atoning sacrifice was made; in his own body, Jesus carried the weight of all of humanity's sins. The penalty for our sin was borne by him. The ransom price was paid in full; the scales of God's divine justice were balanced when Jesus died. So his last word from the cross was a triumphant cry: "It is finished" (John 19:30).

Does it sound strange that Jesus ended all that agonizing misery of body and soul on such a high note? His whole life and mission was to fulfill the Father's will. Jesus knew right from the start that he was on a mission to redeem a lost and condemned world, so he steadfastly set out to accomplish what he had been sent to do. He knew full well the price he would pay.

The night before he died, Jesus pleaded with his Father to find some other way to complete the mission, if at all possible. Yet in the end, Jesus humbly prayed: "Not my will, but yours, be done" (Luke 22:42). And so the Father's will led first to the cross, through pain and death, to victorious resurrection joy.

No wonder, then, that the writer of the letter to the Hebrews frames Christian suffering with joy.

> Let us run with endurance the race that is set before us, looking to Jesus, the founder and perfecter of our faith, who for the joy that was set before him endured the cross, despising the shame, and is seated at the right hand of the throne of God. (Hebrews 12:1–2)

Having finished his race in triumph, Jesus achieved the goal of his entire life and ministry—to pay the penalty for our sin and to ransom humanity from the clutches of sin, death, and hell.

We, too, can find joy in suffering—provided it is wrapped in the suffering of Jesus.

Whether you hurt either physically or emotionally, your suffering will find its meaning in Christ's suffering. Of course, your affliction doesn't pay for anyone's sins, much less your own. That's already over and done: "For our sake [God] made him to be sin who knew no sin, so that in him we might become the righteousness of God" (2 Corinthians 5:21).

Your private pain finds meaning in the collective experience of all of Christ's beloved. Paul, in writing about the suffering he encountered in his ministry, saw affliction as the norm for all Christians. He saw his personal problems as mysteriously linked with the whole church—and the afflictions of Jesus: "Now I rejoice in my sufferings for your sake, and in my flesh I am filling up what is lacking in Christ's afflictions for the sake of his body, that is, the church" (Colossians 1:24).

That's the secret to maintaining an even keel in storm-tossed situations and to finding persistent hope in the midst of your suffering: seeing your affliction as your personal link to Jesus. Because he is "a man of sorrows and acquainted with grief" (Isaiah 53:3), you can be sure you are not alone in your suffering. Jesus is there with you. Because he bore your misery ahead of you and experienced it in a human body just like yours, your pain is sanctified in his. Emotional or physical distress can be endured not because you have sufficient grit and determination to push through it on your own, but because he is alongside you. You have no virtual Savior, but one with flesh and bone and nerve endings just like yours. He knows what he's saying when he invites you to come to him with your worries and burdens: "Come to me, all who labor and are heavy laden, and I will give you rest. Take my yoke upon you, and learn from me, for I am gentle and lowly in heart, and you will find rest for your souls. For my yoke is easy, and my burden is light" (Matthew 11:28–30).

I've seen a lot of suffering in my time. I've been at the bedside of parishioners in agony; I've wrapped my arms around believers collapsing in anguish. I've kept vigil at deathbeds. Once I carried the coffin of a full-term stillborn baby to its tiny grave, grief-stricken parents and clueless young siblings trailing behind me. I've already told you of the chronic physical pain endured daily by both my precious bride and my dearest friend.

This is only a small sampling of the cumulative sorrow and misery in our anguished world: addiction, abuse, disease, loneliness. You can fill in the blank with your own afflictions. Life is never easy; frequently, it's very hard. Occasionally, it seems unbearable. Would you sometimes like to question Jesus about his so-called "easy" yoke and "light" burden?

I won't stop you. I don't want to gloss over your pain, only to help you find your way through it with grace and gratitude. We're getting to that. But for now I would like to stress this single point: you're not alone in your suffering. Jesus goes with you. In drawing close to him you will find comfort in your affliction because Jesus walked your path ahead of you. "For as we share abundantly in Christ's sufferings, so through Christ we share abundantly in comfort too" (2 Corinthians 1:5).

But remember, comfort isn't necessarily *comfortable*. Finding comfort doesn't always mean we are released from suffering. Instead, it means we are not alone in our personal misery or pain; we have company when we hurt. That's what a "comforter" is in the New Testament: someone called alongside us to sustain us in calamity. As Christians, the best we can give each other in times of affliction is what we ourselves have received—comfort from the comforter in chief: Christ Jesus our Lord.

As Paul tells us:

> Blessed be the God and Father of our Lord Jesus Christ, the Father of mercies and God of all comfort.
>
> He comforts us in all our affliction, so that we may be able to comfort those who are in any affliction, with the comfort with which we ourselves are comforted by God.
>
> As we share abundantly in Christ's sufferings, so through Christ we share abundantly in comfort too.
>
> If we are afflicted, it is for your comfort and salvation; and if we are comforted, it is for your comfort.
>
> This you experience when you patiently endure the same sufferings that we suffer.
>
> Our hope for you is unshaken, for we know that as you share in our sufferings, you will also share in our comfort. (2 Corinthians 1:3–7)

He disarmed the rulers
and authorities and put
them to open shame,
by triumphing over
them in the cross.

COLOSSIANS 2:15

V

When You Bear Your Cross, Christ Is Your King

Many Christians have a cross somewhere in their home—a religious plaque, perhaps, or maybe a painting. Some wear crosses around their neck or as other jewelry. Others have a cross tattooed into their skin. These crosses mean different things to different people, I suppose, but all crosses have one thing in common: they distill the essence of our faith. Whether an empty cross or a crucifix, bearing the image of the crucified Redeemer, every cross captures the core of the Christian hope. Because Jesus Christ was crucified and has risen from the dead, there is forgiveness as well as the promise of resurrection into life everlasting for every believing sinner.

The cross is the sign of our salvation.

To preach Christ is always to preach his cross. As the apostle Paul reminded the Corinthians: "And I, when I came to you, brothers, did not come proclaiming to you the testimony of God with lofty speech or wisdom. For I decided to know nothing among you except Jesus Christ and him crucified" (1 Corinthians 2:1–2). The Christian gospel isn't sophisticated; no wonder highbrows so often scorn it. The cross is offensive. It grates on us that God would achieve his highest purpose through lowly degradation and in such disgusting squalor, by using human flesh and bone; nails, spear, and wood; blood, sweat, and spit.

In the gospel that Jesus proclaims, everything is turned inside out and upside down. In our world, winners take all. In his kingdom, the best take the lowest seat: "Everyone who exalts himself will be humbled, and he who humbles himself will be exalted" (Luke 14:11). Likewise, whoever signs on with Jesus needs a radical attitude adjustment:

> If anyone would come after me, let him deny himself and take up his cross and follow me. For whoever would save his life will lose it, but whoever loses his life for my sake and the gospel's will save it. (Mark 8:34–35)

J ust what does it mean to deny yourself and take up your cross? Some have turned their back on riches and fame and taken up serving the poor and destitute in Jesus' name. Others have given up promising careers in impressive fields and gone to seminary to learn to preach the gospel and pastor churches. Still others contend with physical disability or chronic illness every day of their lives. Some are mocked regularly and ridiculed as bigots or haters because they uphold biblical truth instead of cultural fads. Each of these instances fit into a larger pattern: the Christian life is upside down. It follows the pattern of Jesus' cross. As he won by losing, so we live by dying. In his cross and by his death he won life for us all. So upon his invitation we follow Jesus even though it may bring us suffering, misery, and loss.

For all, the cross is the sign of challenge.

In response to Jesus' call, people in every generation have confessed him boldly in word and deed, no matter the consequences. I remember young Christian martyrs kneeling on an obscure North African beach in their blaze-orange prison uniforms—one vivid picture of the cost of discipleship. That price can be high. But to be a Christian witness doesn't always call for martyrdom. Nor do you need to be a pastor or missionary or social service worker to serve Jesus. Every Christian in his or her daily calling is challenged to put Jesus and his kingdom above every selfish motivation— to deny themselves, in other words—then follow Jesus where he takes them.

No matter your circumstances or daily occupations, Jesus is calling you to follow his lead—even if he takes you to places you would rather not go. Whether you're young or old, married or single, no matter your job or role in society—Jesus' invitation is challenging. "Deny yourself," he says. "Take up your cross and follow me."

Jesus would be easier to follow if he would leave out that part about the cross. But that's the thing about Jesus: he's inseparable from his cross. Self-denial and hardship come together in his discipleship package. You can't sidestep the cross.

Frankly, Jesus wouldn't be much of a Savior without his cross, would he? By his cross and in his death, he rescued us all from the clutches of sin, death, and hell. The cross was the price he paid to free us from that bondage. Because of our sins, we deserve nothing but God's judgment and condemnation, yet by his redeeming death Jesus has canceled out the judgment we deserved. "This he set aside, nailing it to the cross" (Colossians 2:14). Likewise, he has trounced Satan and his demonic horde publicly with his cross. "He disarmed the rulers and authorities and put them to open shame, by triumphing over them in the cross" (Colossians 2:15).[4]

Since Christ Jesus laid down his life for us, forgiveness and a whole eternity of joy and bliss await every believing sinner in the resurrection. The cross isn't so bad if it's the cross of Jesus—for by his cross he has won our salvation.

F inally, the cross is a sign of ownership. Paradoxically, you and I find new hope through the crosses that come our way. If we were to continue merrily along, indulging our selfish inclinations, we would find ourselves not only alienated from those we love but estranged from God himself. So when you encounter hardship as a Christian, I'm sure you will discover—as I have found—that the cross can be God's instrument of healing love in your life.

Sometimes he needs to put you in a tight spot to draw you closer to him. Over and over again, I've seen that happen in my own life and in the lives of others I've cared for. I know that sounds counterintuitive. But when you remember that what seems backward and upside down to us is actually right-side up with Jesus, it makes perfect sense. What looked like tragedy at Calvary was triumph in disguise. Though the enemies of Jesus mocked him in his death, he won eternal victory by what looked like defeat, routing all of Satan's hordes with his cross.

It's similar with your cross. In winning, you lose—but in losing for Jesus' sake, you win. You'll be humbled—but Jesus lifts up the lowly. In giving you receive; in pardoning you are pardoned. And in dying you are born to eternal life.

So don't be surprised to discover that when you're down and out, you can see what really matters more clearly. If you're looking for an anchor in the storms of life, look to Christ Jesus, who bought you with his blood and cross. You'll get to know him better when you experience what it means to deny yourself, then take up your cross to follow the path he sets before you. You will discover, as I have, that the way of the cross—though frequently frightening—leads home.

To know Jesus and experience the power of his resurrection here and now, we must share in his sufferings, becoming like him in his death. In the end we will each take our place in glory in the resurrection of all the faithful (Philippians 3:10–11).

First the cross, to be sure. But then the crown. Thanks be to God!

Be gracious to me,
O LORD,
for I am languishing;
heal me, O LORD,
for my bones
are troubled.

Psalm 6:2

VI

When You Are Weak, Christ Is Your Strength

D ifficult days can sneak up on you. Everything is going well, but suddenly you find yourself in the pits. Those stormy stretches sometimes linger for quite a while—often, in my experience, the storms follow each other in rapid sequence. Likely you, too, know how that feels: hardships and uncertainties, losses and calamities keep coming, one after another.

You begin to wonder if you've been targeted for disaster. As my wife likes to jest: "Just because you're paranoid doesn't mean the world isn't out to get you." Distressing times present a problem for the faithful Christian, who knows that our lives aren't random chaos. This is our Father's world, after all. Our loving God made the universe and everything in it. He hasn't gone on an extended vacation, leaving us on our own. As Jesus taught, nothing happens by blind chance: not even a sparrow falling from its nest escapes the Father's notice (Matthew 10:29).

Great minds in philosophy and theology have wrestled with this issue for millennia: If God is good, why is there evil? Logically we might conclude that either God is not good or that he's powerless to do anything about evil.

That's where logic would lead us astray. The cosmic riddle of evil cannot be solved using human reason and our unaided senses. Rather, as we undergo the reality of human calamity and pain, we need to be guided by the Holy Spirit through his word: ultimately, you don't solve suffering—you endure it.

Suffering is natural for the Christian; it's sure to come your way. However, you needn't suffer all alone.

S uffering in itself is a bad thing; let's remember that. Christians are not masochists, looking for suffering wherever they can find it to somehow impress God or others. We Christians should take an unvarnished approach to reality. We shouldn't deemphasize pain or dilute suffering. We ought never call evil good any more than we would call good evil.

So there's nothing wrong with avoiding suffering and trying to relieve pain. We should commend health professionals who facilitate healing for people who suffer physically or mentally. Over the years I've pointed plenty of loved ones and parishioners to them. In their darkest days, suffering people need skilled physicians of mind and body to obtain whatever measure of relief they can find.

If you're stuck in a tight spot, please do reach out for healing help. And while you're at it, look for a spiritual physician, too. The attentive ears and heart of a caring pastor can soothe your aching soul in times of calamity. God has healing gifts for all his saints in his sure word and holy sacraments—seek out such care.

And please, for God's sake, remember this: if you're imperiled emotionally or strung out spiritually, don't conclude there's something wrong with your faith. If you're a pastor or companion to a suffering soul, never belittle their pain or give the impression that their situation isn't bad. Your calling in times of calamity is not to paint smiley faces on human misery. Don't discount suffering and pain of any kind. You can't wave a wand and make ugliness magically disappear. So let's call a spade a spade: Misery upsets. Fear paralyzes. Sickness wearies. Pain hurts. And the most searing pain of all, the final indignation: death stings.

The mystery: God hides himself in the midst of sorrow and distress. Just ask Jeremiah, God's prophet to Judah. If you've read Jeremiah's prophecy, you'll know why he's often called "the weeping prophet." It was his misfortune to serve as God's spokesman through some of the most turbulent times in the history of his people. Jeremiah's earnest appeal to turn from their habitual idolatry and adultery and return to the God of their salvation repeatedly fell on deaf ears. Ultimately, because of their hardened hearts and open rebellion, Judah was sent into captivity in Babylon.

The book of Lamentations, which reflects Judah's calamitous experience in Babylon, is usually attributed to Jeremiah. Though often overlooked, it offers a rich balm for suffering souls. It's a literary work of art, an elaborate poetic expression of lament—filing a complaint with God. The five chapters of this poignant lament reach their epitome squarely in the middle of the book, in chapter three: human calamity eloquently summed up in sixty-six exquisite verses.

The prophet pulls no punches and minces no words as he paints human calamity. As far as suffering people can tell, God alternately seems like a tormentor, a jailer, a hunter, a wild bear, or a ravenous lion looking for prey to devour. Meanwhile, sufferers subsist on bitterness and wormwood, taunted continually by insults and ridicule, treated like scum and garbage. The brutal honesty of Lamentations 3 is not for the faint of heart.

> I have been hunted like a bird
>> by those who were my enemies without
>>> cause;
> they flung me alive into the pit
>> and cast stones on me;
> water closed over my head;
>> I said, "I am lost."
>>>> (Lamentations 3:52–54)

If you've got the stomach to digest the whole cumulative deluge of human affliction encapsulated in these sixty-six raw verses, you will not only hear overtones of Judah's captivity and the voice of the weeping prophet Jeremiah but also echoes of the cry of dereliction from the cross of Calvary, where

Jesus—the man of sorrows—died a tortured death, bearing our sin and shame in his own body.

At the very heart of this rushing torrent of pain stand the following key, visceral lines, powerfully evoking God's tender care for his wounded people:

> Though he cause grief, he will have
> compassion
> according to the abundance of his
> steadfast love;
> for he does not afflict from his heart
> or grieve the children of men.
>
> (Lamentations 3:32–33)

That's the awe-filled secret concealed within affliction: God is right there in the middle of it.

Ever since Eden, God has disguised himself to get closer to us mortal beings. He hides his glory in shame, his power in weakness, his riches in poverty, his majesty in lowliness. We can see this most clearly in the incarnation of God's eternal Son in human flesh. Christ's divinity is wrapped in humanity, his life enclosed within his death. It sounds weird, but that's God for you: he deliberately wraps his faithfulness around those of us who are in misery. As Paul put it: "God chose what is foolish in the world to shame the wise; God chose what is weak in the world to shame the strong;

God chose what is low and despised in the world, even things that are not, to bring to nothing things that are" (1 Corinthians 1:27–28).

F red Rogers, of *Mr. Rogers' Neighborhood*, came out of retirement to comfort traumatized children after the terrorist attack in New York in 2001. "Look for the helpers," he told them. When our lives turn catastrophic, pay more attention to those who are rushing into the trauma than those who are fleeing it.

As much as you and I would like to escape suffering, sooner or later dark days will come to all of us. When those days arrive, it's essential that we not yield to the inevitable panic. We can find grace and gratitude in times of calamity when we see that Christ himself is the helper rushing in. We were lost and without hope; he rushed from heaven to earth, all the way into our frail flesh, to intervene and save us. He rushed into death itself and then further down—even into the death of the cross. But by that death, he conquered death and vanquished hell.

As a result, the darkest valleys of your life can also hold hope. Since he himself was wrapped in lowliness and degradation in his suffering, he is able to comfort you. He knows your suffering intimately well. After all, "we do not have a high priest who is unable to sympathize with our weaknesses, but one who in every respect has been tempted as we are, yet without sin. Let us then with confidence draw near to the throne of grace, that we may receive mercy and find grace to help in time of need" (Hebrews 4:15–16).

In your sorrow and distress you have a Helper who's been there ahead of you. Jesus embraced your pain and misery and sanctified it at the cross by the touch of his sacred body, given for you. Whenever trauma comes your way, Jesus rushes to your side to help with his comforting word. He will never leave you forsaken in your suffering. Be consoled by his sure promise: "I am the resurrection and the life. Whoever believes in me, though he die, yet shall he live, and everyone who lives and believes in me shall never die. Do you believe this?" (John 11:25–26).

Martha answered "yes" that day in Bethany. You can, too. But Jesus knows our every weakness, and this reply will work as well: "Yes Lord; I believe. Help me with my unbelief."

Blessed are
those who mourn,
for they shall be
comforted.

MATTHEW 5:4

VII

When You Are Sad, Christ Is Your Joy

Tragedy happens. We might as well face it. We will encounter dark valleys in our lives. Not continually, thank God. But along with the days of sunshine will come long stretches of darkness. Unfortunately some people seem to have more dark days than others; maybe you're among them. In a way, this chapter is especially for you. It raises the important question of joy: What is it? Where can it be found—especially in the middle of sadness, when there's no happiness in sight?

To find a path through sadness and adversity, you'll need to quit relying on your own inner resources to find it. Instead you'll need to look to God's word to guide you.

The word of God always does what it says. His word is active and powerful—God creates things by simply speaking them into existence. He merely spoke, "Let there be light," and immediately light shone into the black emptiness of the initial creation (Genesis 1:2). You and I describe things with our words, but God's word makes things. That's what sets God's word apart from human language. I can tell you "don't worry," but that doesn't mean a lot. When Jesus says, "Come to me, all who labor and are heavy laden, and I will give you rest," he actually lifts our burdens, calms our weary souls, and soothes our frazzled hearts (Matthew 11:28). The difference, of course, lies in who is speaking. I'm just another person like you, but Jesus is actually God in human flesh. And that makes all the difference in the world.

God's word does what it says. It transforms sinners into saints by the forgiveness of their sins. It changed meaningless chaos into order at creation, and his word can do the same for you. When you wrestle through personal tragedy and turmoil, it creates inner peace by prayerful meditation on what God tells you instead of what you tell yourself. Instead of obsessing over your fears, listen to Jesus instead: "Peace I leave with you; my peace I give to you. Not as the world gives do I give to you. Let not your hearts be troubled, neither let them be afraid" (John 14:27).

If you want to make headway through stormy seas, fix your troubled heart on God's word instead of on your inner feelings. Read his word out loud, silencing your relentless mental rehearsal of your inmost fears. Then pray out loud as well, relieving your pent-up private pain while giving voice to your complaints as you pour out your heart before him. Please note: this inner peace I'm talking about is not just putting on your game face. Prayerful meditation isn't about pretending everything's fine when it's not. It's not about developing resilience by getting through tough spots using your inner resolve and determination. You can get through for a while by pretending. But you'll wear yourself out—first emotionally, then physically. Ultimately, you'll be a spiritual wreck as well. Masks are fine for preventing respiratory infection, but life is no masquerade; honesty is always your best policy.

Tragically, we often carry bravely on trying to mask our true feelings. Like Anna in the classic American musical *The King and I*, we whistle a happy tune outwardly while inwardly there's no happiness to be found. "Whenever I feel afraid," she sang, "I whistle a happy tune and every single time the happiness in that tune convinces me that I'm not afraid." That charade comes with a high price tag, though. It takes a lot of emotional energy to fake happiness when all you've got inside is fear and sadness.

Life is too short to keep faking it. Christians don't need to pretend that tragedies never happen or suffering isn't miserable or pain doesn't hurt. We can afford to be honest with God, because he knows the depth of human suffering. We can confidently cry out to him from the bottom of our anxious hearts, knowing we have a Father in heaven who shows compassion to his children (Psalm 103:13). We have a Savior who wept at the grave of his dear friend Lazarus (John 11:35). When we're at a loss for words, the Holy Spirit takes over, interceding for us himself (Romans 8:26).

God tenderly invites our prayers, promising his attentive ear: "Call upon me in the day of trouble; I will deliver you, and you shall glorify me" (Psalm 50:15). There's no need to pretend that we're happy when we're not. Happiness is often in short supply in this world; it comes and goes depending on the circumstances. But joy? That's a whole different matter. Joy abounds in every circumstance if we just have eyes to see it.

We'll need to sort out the difference between joy and happiness. Happiness depends largely on our experiences. It fluctuates with our emotional state—a sort of barometer for our emotions, you might say. In contrast, joy is firmly rooted in God and his promises. That's why it remains steady despite the ups and downs of life.

I'll admit, I'm partial to happiness. If you offer me a glass half full and a glass half empty, I'll pick the first one every time—especially if it's half full of my favorite wine. I enjoy my family and the company of good friends. I like bright sunny days and blue skies, fine music and good times. I prefer fulfilling and satisfying experiences as much as anyone. Happiness is great while it lasts. But that's just it—happiness doesn't last. It's here today and gone tomorrow. It's momentary and fleeting. Just when you think total happiness is finally within your reach, it slips out of your grip. Happiness ebbs and flows with the seasons of life. Recent years have brought that home for me as I've discovered that aging isn't always fun.

Yet joy remains even when happiness fades. No matter the circumstance, Christians who plant their hope in God can harvest genuine joy in the rocky soil of adversity or in the deepest, darkest valley of pain. Joy and faith are linked, writes the apostle James:

Count it all joy, my brothers, when you meet trials of various kinds, for you know that the testing of your faith produces steadfastness. And let steadfastness have its full effect, that you may be perfect and complete, lacking in nothing. (James 1:2–4)

See what James did there? "Count it all joy," he advises. James is no fool. The life of the disciples was no walk in the park. If we are to believe tradition, only one of them—John—died in bed, while all the rest met violent deaths at the hands of persecutors. From their own canonical writings as well as the testimonies of their contemporaries, they faced opposition at every turn, hounded by the enemies of the gospel inside and outside the church. So for James, joy was an exercise in faith. "Count it all joy," he says. All those *trials of various kinds* he chalked up under the "joy" column in his life, even though those trials robbed him of happiness.

That's quite a trick. Isn't that merely playing mind games? Another version of pretending? James wouldn't say so. He goes on to say that these trials are actually God's testing program. When you test positive for faith, it's a very good thing. Faith was first planted in you by the Holy Spirit, and it grows steadfast under fire, strengthening your grip on Jesus and his cross. In the end such growing steadfastness will bring to fruition what God first began in you by his grace.

Never be afraid to give voice to your deepest distress when in the darkest valleys of your life. God is actively at work even there, producing in you what is well-pleasing in his sight. Sadly, calamity is bound to come your way in this broken world. When tragedy happens, it's easy to lose your way. We're walking here by faith, after all, and the sadness all around you obstructs your view of the Lord, who bought you with his blood. Peter helps us see the whole picture clearly: "Though you have not seen him, you love him. Though you do not now see him, you believe in him and rejoice with joy that is inexpressible and filled with glory" (1 Peter 1:8).

So Christ and calamity are bound together within the grace of God. Trusting his sure word, he will see you through your present sadness into everlasting joy on the day of his coming.

Even the darkness
is not dark to you;
the night is bright as
the day, for darkness
is as light with you.

PSALM 139:12

VIII

When You Are in Darkness, Christ Is Your Light

Seeing is believing, they say. Thomas would agree. That first Easter evening, when Jesus appeared in living flesh and blood to his amazed disciples, Thomas wasn't there. When they told him what they had seen, he was incredulous: "Unless I see in his hands the mark of the nails, and place my finger into the mark of the nails, and place my hand into his side, I will never believe" (John 20:25).

We understand Thomas, don't we? His reaction reflects our own experience: dead people don't walk and talk. It makes sense that Thomas would want to see Jesus with his own eyes. I think I would, too.

Eight days later, Thomas got his proof.

The disciples were again together in that same locked room, and this time Thomas was among them. The risen Lord suddenly appeared again. "Put your finger here," Jesus said, indicating the nail marks in his hands. He invited Thomas, "Put out your hand, and place it in my side," showing his flesh wound. "Do not disbelieve, but believe" (John 20:27).

And Thomas called him "God." "My Lord and my God," he confessed. Jesus responded, "Have you believed because you have seen me? Blessed are those who have not seen and yet have believed" (John 20:29).

That's where you and I come in. More than twenty centuries separate us from that night when Jesus appeared, alive, to his astonished disciples. We've never laid eyes on Jesus or touched his living body with our own hands. Yet Jesus tells us there's a blessing for people like us, who believe without seeing him.

Remember this blessing when you walk through the dark days that are sure to come into your life.

That darkness comes in all sizes and shapes. When you wrestle with chronic worry or pass through deep valleys of anguish, grief, or despair, it's hard to cling to God's promises. If your body is also wracked with pain, it's hard to think straight, let alone pray. If your mind is locked in trauma mode and you're hit with panic attacks, it's hard to focus on anything else. If your heart is pounding and your head is reeling, it's hard to think of God, much less pray.

Faith is weak at these times. Sometimes it's just hanging by a thread. Yet faith is faith, and if you believe in Jesus in those darkest valleys of your distress, you are blessed. Jesus said so himself!

"Now we see in a mirror dimly," Paul wrote, "but then face to face" (1 Corinthians 13:12). What we will one day see with our own risen eyes in eternal glory, we can already dimly see by faith.

Unfortunately what we perceive by faith is often clouded in anxiety and murky with fear. Anxiety and fear frequently merge into doubt—and occasionally something worse. Suffering saints through the centuries have told of dark nights of the soul when God seems absent and unresponsive. In those fearful times, hope begins to fade and faith grows dim. Over the years I've guided a handful of people through such episodes, which can be shockingly traumatic. Yet even in such dark nights, Jesus' blessing holds firm: "Blessed are those who have not seen and yet have believed."

But what should we do when the future is uncertain and faith seems futile? When God seems far away? What can we do when fear takes over and sorrow overwhelms us?

Where can we find light in our own dark nights?

The psalmist guides our way. King David voices the anguished cry of every suffering saint who has ever wondered if God is absent:

> Where shall I go from your Spirit?
>> Or where shall I flee from your presence?
> If I ascend to heaven, you are there!
>> If I make my bed in Sheol, you are there!
> If I take the wings of the morning
>> and dwell in the uttermost parts of the sea,
> even there your hand shall lead me,
>> and your right hand shall hold me.
>
> (Psalm 139:7–10)

God is present everywhere, even when our human eyes do not detect him. Though we cannot see him, he sees us. Were we to climb to the heights of heaven, descend to the depths of hell, or fly away to the farthest seas, his gracious presence would still be there. Even when we feel abandoned, he is present with us every moment of every day.

In stormy seas of uncertainty and deep, dark valleys of despair, when we sense nothing but fear and dread, his hand still leads and his love still supports us. Through every long and lonely night of misery God himself stands guard, holding us safe and secure. Darkness is no threat to him.

> If I say, "Surely the darkness shall cover me,
>   and the light about me be night,"
> even the darkness is not dark to you;
>   the night is bright as the day,
>   for darkness is as light with you.
>
> (Psalm 139:11–12)

No doubt you've had your share of long, dark nights; most Christians have. Grief, or pain, or loss of one sort or another will bring those times of darkness into your life. When you can't sleep, your body's telling you your mind is on overload and your heart is breaking. Some nights it's hard to pray, and when you do it seems like no one's there to listen. In that darkness, you will feel that God is gone and your own misery is your only company.

My personal darkest nights came after our young son-in-law tragically died in a farm accident. For several nights in a row, my body shook with wrenching silent sobs while my heart cried out, "Why, God, why? What will our precious daughter and their little boy do now?" You know that prayer; very likely you've prayed one like it yourself. Although this wonderful world God made for us contains a lot of beauty and happiness, it also holds a lot of ugliness. And sorrow. And fear. And pain. And death.

But remember, we serve a Lord who snatched life from the jaws of death. He brought light into darkness. One Friday afternoon at Calvary, darkness enveloped Jesus while he suffered extreme agony of body, mind, and spirit upon his cross. After three anguished hours of torture, he breathed his last, and his friends took his battered, bloodied body down and buried him in a borrowed tomb.

In a physical body—just like ours—Jesus bore our sin and carried our sorrows.

The price of our sins was paid in human flesh and bone, blood, sweat, and tears. Jesus experienced pain like ours. Fear and dread came upon him just like it does on us, and he felt our human anguish with every fiber of his being.

But by his cross and in the death that he died, Christ Jesus brought life and immortality. Three days later he emerged from his grave victorious over death and hell, transforming this world's darkness into everlasting light.

Although you may spend long hours in anguished prayer wondering if God is even there to hear you, you can be sure that your private darkness is not dark to him. Night is bright as day to him, and darkness is as light (Psalm 139:12). He sees clearly in the dark. And you can be sure he will hold you, safe. "He knows what is in the darkness, and the light dwells with him" (Daniel 2:22).

When you were baptized you were born again, into a living hope through the resurrection of Jesus Christ from the dead (1 Peter 1:3). Now your life is securely anchored in the living flesh and blood of your crucified Lord.

True, you haven't seen Jesus for yourself like Thomas, nor have you traced the print of the nails in his hands or touched the wound in his living flesh. But you do believe in him nonetheless, and so you are blessed. Jesus said so.

Though your nights are unbearably long and your darkness impenetrably deep, Christ Jesus will sustain you and see you through them. You may not see him now, but you will see him soon enough—on the day of the resurrection of all flesh. Then all sorrow and sighing will flee away, and death will be no more. God will wipe away your every tear with his own hand. Then you will enter into the eternal joy of your master, a joy no one will ever be able to take away.

Though you have not seen him, you love him. Though you do not now see him, you believe in him and rejoice with joy that is inexpressible and filled with glory, obtaining the outcome of your faith, the salvation of your souls. (1 Peter 1:8–9)

In the deepest valleys of your life, through every long and dark night, in every trouble, you can call upon Christ Jesus. Pour out your complaints to him. Pray, praise, and give him thanks. His promise stands forever sure: "I am yours and you are mine, and there is nothing that can ever separate me from you or you from me."

The grass withers,
the flower fades,
but the word of our God
will stand forever.

ISAIAH 40:8

IX

When You Are Alone, Christ Is with You

Nothing lasts forever. You and I know that rationally, but emotionally we would rather not face it. And we aren't the first generation to avoid this truth: early Spanish explorers came to these shores looking for the fabled fountain of youth. In America we've commercialized their search and made it into a science. Health clubs, diet systems, and exercise programs are lucrative ventures for entrepreneurs to cash in on America's perpetual quest for beautiful bodies and youthful vigor.

Don't get me wrong, health and fitness are important. But many of us are in denial. Though we know we're not immortal, we prefer to live as if we are. The thought of giving up familiar daily work in retirement is bad enough, but dying?

That's off our radar! So each generation mimics the generation after it. Grandparents pretend sixty is the new forty. Most of us actually come to believe we're younger than we really are. So we keep pushing off the inevitable.

Optimism has its place but only accompanied by a healthy dose of realism. Sooner or later we're all going to die, unless the Lord Jesus returns to usher in his eternal kingdom. The psalmist sets us straight with a jolt of reality:

> Lord, you have been our dwelling place
> > in all generations.
> Before the mountains were brought forth,
> > or ever you had formed the earth and the
> > > world,
> > from everlasting to everlasting you are God.
> You return man to dust
> > and say, "Return, O children of man!"
> For a thousand years in your sight
> > are but as yesterday when it is past,
> > or as a watch in the night.
> You sweep them away as with a flood; they
> > > are like a dream,
> > like grass that is renewed in the morning:
> in the morning it flourishes and is renewed;
> > in the evening it fades and withers.
>
> (Psalm 90:1–6)

In this psalm we are forced to face facts. "Here today and gone tomorrow" is no cliché; it accurately sums up the transience of human life.

In comparison to the vastness of eternity, the passing of a thousand years is nothing; our own short lives are even less. We need to face the relentless course of decline and decay. Just as grass that thrives in the morning dew is cut down that same evening for cattle fodder, in this fallen world we humans are born to die. Like it or not, this is our common destiny after Eden.

The prophet Isaiah paints a similar picture of human decay and death, but he then injects God's promise of eternal hope.

> All flesh is grass,
>> and all its beauty is like the flower
>>> of the field.
> The grass withers, the flower fades
>> when the breath of the LORD
>>> blows on it;
>> surely the people are grass.
> The grass withers, the flower fades,
>> but the word of our God will stand forever.
>>>> (Isaiah 40:6–8)

Something in this world lasts forever, after all.

True enough; human life is fragile. We're all just one short breath and a few feeble heartbeats away from death at any given moment. Some of us put our lives at risk routinely, but thankfully most of us don't often have a reason to think seriously about dying.

But that can change in an instant. Sometimes the specter of death breaks in on us suddenly and intensely—a tragic accident, perhaps. A violent crime. A dire illness. Any number of calamities can suddenly bring us face-to-face with mortality. In one horrific moment, our resilience dissipates. We find it impossible to remain serene and calm when facing death—our own or that of those we love.

Nothing lasts forever. If we want stability, we'll need to find an anchor outside this turbulent world.

The prophet Isaiah writes, "The word of our God will stand forever." Because God himself is eternal, his word lasts to all eternity. Nothing else endures.

Check your mirror: have you noticed a stray gray hair showing up unexpectedly or unwelcome wrinkles appearing? We seem surprised that we grow older, as though somehow we can avoid the passage of time.

We should know better, of course. Most adults notice how children seem to grow by inches every passing month and how suddenly babies turn into toddlers. But for some reason we think that when we at last arrive at the prime of life, we're going to stay there permanently. In this decaying world, nobody gets a pass on death.

It's not only the frail elderly who die. I've buried little children as well as women and men in the prime of life—I've already told you about my beloved son-in-law. No doubt death has touched you, too; you likely already know intimately the pain of loss and the grueling ache of grief.

Here's the unvarnished truth: death is here to stay until Jesus returns to claim his bride, the church. On that final day he will raise all the saints in the power of his resurrection, out of the dust of death into risen eternal glory. But Jesus has not abandoned us until then. We aren't just biding our time, running out the clock in this dying world. We have an anchor in eternity. Jesus promises to be with us every step of the way, even in calamity and the darkest valleys of our lives. He ties his eternal presence to his living and abiding word.

J esus told Peter, "The words that I have spoken to you are spirit and life" (John 6:63). When tragedy interrupts our lives or adversity strikes, we need to listen to Jesus. He links his life-giving Spirit to the words he speaks.

Peter was listening carefully. So when Jesus asked his disciples if they were going to leave—like many others who rejected his teaching—Peter spoke for them all. "Lord, to whom shall we go?" he said. "You have the words of eternal life" (John 6:68).

Perhaps in your own personal world, facing decline and loss, you've begun to wonder if Jesus has abandoned you to muddle through as best you can. When everything seems stacked against you, people often begin to think that God is against them, too. Whether you've faced long days of ongoing distress or one short hour of deep darkness, you might sense you've been abandoned by both God and everyone you know. Don't believe it for a minute. Christ Jesus has promised to be with you in his abiding word of grace and hope.

All this calls for faith, of course. But in the deepest valleys and most anxious moments of life, faith is frequently in short supply. Where will you find the faith you need to survive and thrive? The same place you find Jesus: in his word. "Faith comes from hearing, and hearing through the word of Christ" (Romans 10:17).

See how that works? Instead of retreating into your head to cope with misery, you need to get out of yourself. In stressful times fears and doubts cycle endlessly through our minds in a continuous loop of anxiety and distress. Break that ugly cycle. Find a quiet place where you can talk out loud. Open up your Bible, and read aloud the words of Jesus. His words are Spirit and life.

Those very words of Jesus will give you the faith you need to speak aloud your prayers and praises, petitions and thanksgivings. Don't hold anything back. In his calming presence you can pour out the contents of your anguished heart in confident prayer.

There's only one place to be when calamity strikes or the darkness of this decaying world engulfs you in its fearful grip. Isolation is your enemy—there's no way to tackle personal distress or public tragedy alone. But you don't need to. Go to Jesus; he has the words of eternal life.

And those words are life for you.

To me to live is Christ,
and to die is gain.

PHILIPPIANS 1:21

X

When You Are Dying, Christ Is Your Life

Do you remember that children's nursery-rhyme game called "ring around the rosy"? You joined hands with your friends and moved around in a circle, chanting the words:

Ring around the rosy
Pockets full of posy
Ashes! Ashes!
We all fall down.

At the last line, the goal was to see who could fall down first. You certainly didn't want to be the last one standing. As far as we knew when we were children, these lines were harmless nonsense. Like all classic nursery rhymes, their exact meaning lies buried under generations of folklore. But some speculate the game originated during the Middle

Ages, mocking some deadly plague. A rose-colored ring on the skin was the first infection symptom; small posies of flowers and herbs were thought to ward off death. And ashes and falling down? The grim final outcome of the disease.

It may seem morbid to our enlightened generation that children back then would make death into child's play. But I think our reaction would say more about our world than theirs. We hold death at arm's length, avoiding the topic as much as possible.

In contrast, the Scriptures speak frequently about death. And yet we Christians too easily embrace our culture's unhealthy phobia when it comes to death. We're embarrassed to mention it. We've taken to adopting the circumlocutions of our day to get around death and dying. We treat dead bodies as empty receptacles to be discarded. We speak of the dead as the "departed." We like to call funerals "celebrations of life." We prefer cremation to in-ground burial.

We should be cautious about this, however. Many customs exist when it comes to burial practices, and some have valid reasons for cremation. Grieving is personal, and we shouldn't make pronouncements where God hasn't given us directives. But we also need to talk more frequently and candidly about foundational Christian beliefs about death.

Biblically speaking, death is an enemy. It's an outrageous intrusion into God's perfect creation. God forbade our first parents from accessing Eden's tree of the knowledge of good and evil. "In the day that you eat of it you shall surely die" (Genesis 2:17). But eat they did. And die they did. They and their children after them and so on down to this very day, each succeeding generation in turn succumbs to the consequences of that first and original sin from which all other sins flow.

Death is most certainly not child's play. Death is neither to be scrupulously avoided or casually embraced. People speak about "death with dignity" without acknowledging that death is the ultimate indignation—a division between body and soul, the separation of breath from flesh.

But that separation is not permanent. That's what I want to stress—I want to get you ready to die. Does that shock you? I assure you, I mean no disrespect. Throughout the centuries the church has always had a healthy respect for dying people. And the truth is, we're all dying.

From the youngest newborn to the eldest nursing-home patient, we're all in the process of dying.

Preparing for death is part of Christian living. Our ancestors in the faith were concerned that fellow believers be prepared for what they called a "blessed death"—falling asleep in faith in the sure and certain hope of the resurrection unto eternal life in Jesus Christ our Lord.

While we need to find consolation and comfort in Christ for every calamity that comes our way, our ultimate need for consolation and comfort in him is when we come to the end of life. And then, the spotlight is continually on Christ Jesus. He remains the Way, the Truth, and the Life both in life and death. "If we live, we live to the Lord, and if we die, we die to the Lord. So then, whether we live or whether we die, we are the Lord's" (Romans 14:8).

As our brother in our human flesh, Jesus has already conquered death. His physical body was the instrument of our salvation. In skin and bones like ours, he bore our sin. He suffered excruciating agony of body and soul upon his cross. Three days later his resurrection was the culmination of our redemption, but it all began with his crucifixion. Like bookends, they encapsulate the whole package of our deliverance: death and resurrection, cross and empty tomb. Because he emerged victorious from his grave and conquered death, we will too.

In flesh and blood like ours, Jesus destroyed death and ransacked hell. His human body was the bait that Satan swallowed at Calvary, plotting to destroy God's anointed. But Jesus' divine nature was the hook that destroyed the devil and robbed him of all his power, delivering us from bondage to sin, death, and hell.[5]

> Since therefore the children share in flesh and blood, he himself likewise partook of the same things, that through death he might destroy the one who has the power of death, that is, the devil, and deliver all those who through fear of death were subject to lifelong slavery. (Hebrews 2:14–15)

Jesus defeated death by his own death. Satan sought to be the devourer, but he ended up being the one devoured—because God cannot die. As God, Jesus is life, and so death has no power over him. Jesus—who is both God and man—suffered and died and rose again in his human body. With his flesh and blood intact, he destroyed death and made captivity captive.

The waters of baptism join Christians to Jesus' cross and resurrection, by which he won victory over death and hell. "We were buried therefore with him by baptism into death, in order that, just as Christ was raised from the dead by the glory of the Father, we too might walk in newness of life" (Romans 6:4).

That life is now yours. Having died with Christ in baptism, you also live with him. And you can count on that life in Christ to sustain you every single day of your life. That includes days of darkness and pain as well as days of sunshine and happiness.

In a very real way, having been baptized into Christ, you have put on Christ. You live in him, and he in you. Paul writes: "I have been crucified with Christ. It is no longer I who live, but Christ who lives in me. And the life I now live in the flesh I live by faith in the Son of God, who loved me and gave himself for me" (Galatians 2:20).

That changes everything for the Christian facing death. Baptized into Christ's death, you have already gotten death out of the way. You might say the grave has been defanged. All of death's power to destroy has already been annihilated by Jesus' death and resurrection. As Jesus rested in his tomb for three days before his glorious rising on Easter day, so the Christian falls asleep in this world only to be raised with all the saints with body and soul intact in eternal glory.

Our hope remains consistently rooted in Christ and his sure word through good times and bad. Christ Jesus holds us safe throughout. In times of joy and peace, in times of suffering and pain, in times of distress and catastrophe, our security rests in Jesus' blood and righteousness. He is the solid rock; all else in life is sinking sand. Commend yourself always into his care—you've got nothing to lose and everything to gain. You can say with Paul: "For to me to live is Christ, and to die is gain" (Philippians 1:21).

This doesn't change the fact that death is a fearful prospect. But remember: you are baptized into Christ, and so you have already died, as far as sin and death are concerned. You have only life to look forward to—here and now, every day you live on earth, and hereafter in heaven's joyful peace.

To help us get ready, we have a dress rehearsal every night as we lie down to sleep in anticipation of rising in the morning.

> Teach me to live that I may dread
> the grave as little as my bed.
> Teach me to die that so I may
> Rise glorious at the awefull day.[6]

Dark nights and deep valleys go with the territory in this world of sin. Long days of suffering and plenty of anxious fear may be in store for you. But there are better days ahead. A whole eternity of glory, in fact: "The sufferings of this present time are not worth comparing with the glory that is to be revealed to us" (Romans 8:18).

One of the things people fear most about death is the prospect of dying alone. But if you are a Christian, know this: Christ Jesus, who bore your sin and carried your sorrows in his own body into death and buried them in his tomb, now lives forever in risen glory. Because he died and was raised again, he has removed the sting of death and brought life and immortality to light for all the faithful.

On the day you die, I guarantee you won't be alone in that day and hour. Jesus will be there to guide you through the perils of death and the grave into the bright courts of heaven's glory, where he already lives and reigns with the Father and the Holy Spirit, one God now and forever.

You were slain, and
by your blood
you ransomed
people for God from
every tribe and language
and people and nation,
and you have made them
a kingdom and priests
to our God, and
they shall reign
on the earth.

REVELATION 5:10–11

XI

Christ Is Your Victory

Christ and calamity certainly go together. Though we all face calamities, we often don't know what to do with them when they come. The frightened disciples looked to Jesus, only to find him asleep in the stern of their storm-tossed boat. They called out in terror: "Teacher, do you not care that we are perishing?" (Mark 4:38). Their boat was about to go under, and the disciples were out of options. So they called out for help. Suffering and uncertainty will do that to you.

Jesus had a whole discourse for his followers on what to do in tight spots. He explains that since God takes care of all creation, we shouldn't need to fret about our daily needs. The evidence of God's loving care is all around us, he says, chirping in the tree branches and waving in the sunshine.

Look at the birds of the air: they neither sow nor reap nor gather into barns, and yet your heavenly Father feeds them.

Are you not of more value than they?

And which of you by being anxious can add a single hour to his span of life?

And why are you anxious about clothing? Consider the lilies of the field, how they grow: they neither toil nor spin, yet I tell you, even Solomon in all his glory was not arrayed like one of these. (Matthew 6:26–29)

When we are discouraged or afraid in difficult situations, we should follow the example of the disciples during that storm: go to the Lord in prayer.

Prayer has both God's command and God's promise: "Call upon me in the day of trouble; I will deliver you, and you shall glorify me" (Psalm 50:15). For me the first part comes naturally; the last part not so much. I'm quick to call on God for help when I'm in trouble, but I often forget to thank him afterward.

"One day at a time" is essential for any number of self-help and addiction-recovery programs. The phrase contains a lot of practical wisdom. It's foundational to the Lord's Prayer, for example, where Jesus instructs us to pray for what we need day by day: "give us this day our daily bread." Squinting down the road, into the unknown future, is what grips our hearts with fear.

When calamity strikes, we tend to borrow trouble: we slip into panic mode, wondering what's to become of us, worrying incessantly about what lies ahead. When our minds are filled with "oh no" and "why me" and "what if," those questions often crowd out faith in God's loving purpose and care.

In the middle of calamity, it's easy to obsess over looming disaster.

By pointing us to the birds of the air and flowers of the field, Jesus wants to quiet the unnerving anxiety that takes over our minds so easily from day to day—but especially in adversity. "Do not be anxious, saying, 'What shall we eat?' or 'What shall we drink?' or 'What shall we wear?' For the Gentiles seek after all these things, and your heavenly Father knows that you need them all. But seek first the kingdom of God and his righteousness, and all these things will be added to you" (Matthew 6:31–33).

God's kingdom has already arrived, embodied in Jesus and his undying love. His righteousness is ours as well, rooted in his flesh and blood offered upon his cross and freely bestowed in his gospel and sacraments. With these certainties guaranteed, we can face the tribulations of an uncertain future in confident hope. "Therefore do not be anxious about tomorrow, for tomorrow will be anxious for itself. Sufficient for the day is its own trouble" (Matthew 6:34). Each day is sure to bring plenty of worry, heartache, and trouble on its own—no need to borrow trouble from tomorrow.

Jesus teaches us to face our losses and disasters by taking each day as it comes, assured of the blessings he gives us by faith and thus confident in the Father's loving kindness. He does not belittle our fears. He shares our flesh and blood, and so he knows full well that anxiety comes naturally to the human heart. What he tells us instead is not to be anxious about *tomorrow*.

Instead of indulging our worries and anxieties, we can bring them to Jesus instead. He calms our fears and quiets our apprehensions in the bounty of his love—one day at a time.

Prayer is crucial in times of personal or national distress—but our prayer must be coupled with gratitude.

Thankful prayer has been crucial for Christians through the ages. It sustained the early church through periods of persecution and martyrdom. It supported the church through the devastating plagues of the Middle Ages. It has given hope to Christians through the tumultuous decades of the twentieth century, and it is carrying us now, amid the uncertainties of the twenty-first. Thankful prayer will help you too through your darkest days and deepest valleys.

> The Lord is at hand; do not be anxious about anything, but in everything by prayer and supplication with thanksgiving let your requests be made known to God. And the peace of God, which surpasses all understanding, will guard your hearts and your minds in Christ Jesus. (Philippians 4:5–7)

Here Paul unpacks what Jesus taught in his Sermon on the Mount: anxiety is diminished when Christians bring their distress to the Lord, who bought them with his blood. Since he is near at hand, they needn't let fears multiply exponentially. They can voice their distress to God through faith in their Lord Jesus, "by prayer and supplication with thanksgiving."

Maybe the reason we aren't so good at thanking God is that we haven't learned to blend gratitude in with our prayers and supplications. It doesn't come naturally. We tend to wait until calamity resolves and then thank God that it's over and we've survived. But notice: Paul teaches us that thanking God comes first. Intercessions and thanksgivings belong together. Gratitude goes along with grace.

It's hard to be thankful in the midst of distress. We get so overwhelmed by trauma that thanksgiving isn't in the picture. We're so laser-focused on the few things that go horribly wrong each day that we forget the scores of things that go right.

Lots of blessings slip through our sieve because they're so routine. Clothing and shoes, food and drink, house and home, spouse and children, work and income—all these essential things we tend to take for granted and neglect to acknowledge as genuine gifts from God. He gives them purely out of his fatherly, divine goodness and mercy, not due to any merit or worthiness in us.

Above all these earthly gifts we also have the gift of salvation—God's kingdom and righteousness, earned by Christ and freely given to us. That's why thanksgiving goes with prayer.

You've got plenty to pray about. The constant flow of tribulations that come your way in this storm-tossed, sin-weary world calls for constant prayer and supplication. But remember that even in the midst of heartache and misery you've got much to be thankful for.

God's grace in Jesus results in gratitude. "Rejoice always, pray without ceasing, give thanks in all circumstances; for this is the will of God in Christ Jesus for you" (1 Thessalonians 5:16–18). Even amid sadness there is joy in Jesus. He sees us in our worst distress, and he blesses us.

There's an old story about a little boy who was afraid of the dark. One night in the middle of a horrific thunderstorm he cried out in fear, and his father went in to comfort him. "You don't need to be afraid," he said to his son. "Don't you know that Jesus is with you?" "Yes," said the boy. "But I want somebody with skin on."

Can you identify? You and I tend to look to tangible, visible things for security. When we're overwhelmed by the things our eyes can see, we find it hard to focus on something we can't. But Christian hope is focused on spiritual realities that are very, very real. The Lord Jesus has not gone away and left us without testimony. Though we cannot see him with our eyes or touch him with our hands as Thomas did, he does reveal himself to us in his word, in water, in bread and wine. His cross and tomb are far removed from us by history and geography, yet he regularly bestows his gifts of forgiveness, life, and salvation to us in his word and sacrament. But we prefer someone with skin on. We'd rather walk by sight instead of faith.

It isn't easy to keep on keeping on in times of adversity or uncertainty. It's so very easy to lose heart in the life of faith. Losing somebody you love will do that to you. So will losing a job, losing a marriage, or losing your honor and reputation. Based only on what you see, you wonder if God has left you. All you can see is misery and darkness. An aging body, perhaps. A future of uncertainty. An endless landscape of hopeless pain. You begin to think maybe God's gone on an extended vacation to somewhere else in the universe because in your corner of the planet he's nowhere to be found.

My hope is that this book helps you look for God in the right places. Life growing hard doesn't mean that he's left you. Exactly the opposite, really. But you need to know where to look. Just as the divinity of Jesus was hidden in his humanity, just as his glory was openly displayed in the shame and suffering of his cross, so he draws nearest to you in your life's lowest ebb.

In times of calamity, Jesus hasn't left you comfortless, but you'll need to look to things you cannot see for comfort. Outwardly, your life may be in turmoil. Inwardly you can be renewed each day by God's grace provided that you have eyes to see how he is present in your distress.

> So we do not lose heart. Though our outer self is wasting away, our inner self is being renewed day by day. For this light momentary affliction is preparing for us an eternal weight of glory beyond all comparison, as we look not to the things that are seen but to the things that are unseen. For the things that are seen are transient, but the things that are unseen are eternal. (2 Corinthians 4:16–18)

Paul doesn't dismiss human suffering as if it's nothing. True, he does call such affliction "light" and "momentary," but he has in view the weighty joys of God's eternal glory still to come. The key is to concentrate on what human senses can't detect. That's plenty hard when your body is wracked with pain or when you're enduring a string of reversals and hardships that go relentlessly on and on.

But consider this: everything you see around you is fading away. One day soon, when Jesus returns, the suffering and misery of this world will all be gone. "Heaven and earth will pass away, but my words will not pass away" (Matthew 24:35). During any distress pay attention to his life-giving words. Even when your eye can't detect it or your heart can't feel it, God is present with you by his word and Spirit. What you cannot see will sustain you amid the fearful things you see. Things that are seen are transient; only unseen things are eternal.

As we come to the end of this book I want to leave you in good hands: the hands of God. When all is said and done, confidence in the midst of trial and distress is not under your control. Unfortunately this sad world holds a lot of suffering and pain that humanly can't be fixed. Suffering must be suffered. That's the long and the short of it.

Yet it's not just a matter of developing a stiff upper lip. The solution to distress is not somehow to grin and bear it, waiting for a pie in the sky by and by, as skeptics sarcastically caricature the hope of the glories to come. No, there is help in the midst of your anguish.

Anxieties cannot be avoided. You can't just wave them off like you would shoo away a fly. You don't flip some internal switch to deactivate anxiety. Rather, as Peter says, you need to give your anxieties to God, "casting all your anxieties on him, because he cares for you" (1 Peter 5:7). God really does care. His love is not just lip service. God's love led him to give up his only-begotten Son to the death of the cross so that whosoever believes in him will not perish, but have everlasting life.

There's your hope, right there: life everlasting. In this world nothing lasts forever, not even suffering and uncertainties. They will be swept away in the eternal joys of the world to come. This world will pass away, and all of its miseries with it. But God's word will never pass away.

In his word God lets us in on an astonishing secret about the end of time:

> I tell you a mystery. We shall not all sleep, but we shall all be changed, in a moment, in the twinkling of an eye, at the last trumpet. For the trumpet will sound, and the dead will be raised imperishable, and we shall be changed. For the perishable body must put on the imperishable, and this mortal body must put on immortality.
>
> When the perishable puts on the imperishable, and the mortal puts on immortality,

then shall come to pass the saying that is written:

"Death has been swallowed up in victory."

"O death, where is your victory?
    O death, where is your sting?"

The sting of death is sin, and the power of sin is the law. But thanks be to God, who gives us the victory through our Lord Jesus Christ. (1 Corinthians 15:51–57)

Not far from where I live is a beautiful cemetery in the rolling hills of Wisconsin, overlooking a picturesque lake. It has a long history, and its graves hold the remains of the greatest and the least in our little community dating back to the Civil War. It's a lovely place of peace and tranquility.

But deeply etched in my memory of that place is another scene not so peaceful. It was a stunningly gorgeous day late in May, a decade ago. Scores of mourners accompanied our daughter as she laid to rest the body of her young husband, victim of a tragic accident and father of their little boy. Tears flowed freely all around. The grief was raw and visceral. If you've ever buried someone you love, you can grasp that heartbreaking scene in your own mind and heart.

Grieving is a good thing when you grieve in hope of the final consummation ahead. "Blessed are those who mourn, for they shall be comforted," Jesus said (Matthew 5:4). And we were comforted that bitter day. I'll never forget the words of our pastor as he stood at the head of Tim's casket, near the yawning chasm of his grave.

Before the burial rite our pastor calmly told us why we had nothing to fear in this place of death that so many find revolting. The early Christians took their word for the place of the dead from the word for bedroom or sleeping chamber. "Cemeteries" were barracks for the dead in Christ, who waited to be awakened with Christ's return.

We were about to lay our beloved Tim to rest that day, our pastor explained, in anticipation that he would be awakened on the day of the resurrection of all flesh. Our pastor then tucked him in for his final rest, speaking these triumphant words:

> We now commit the body of our brother to the ground; earth to earth, ashes to ashes, dust to dust, in the sure and certain hope of the resurrection to eternal life through our Lord Jesus Christ, who will change our

lowly bodies so that they will be like His glorious body, by the power that enables Him to subdue all things to Himself.[7]

There it is. The death and resurrection of Jesus Christ our Lord. That's your hope in a world of hopelessness.

Because Christ Jesus your Lord was given over into death for you, what you see in this world is not what you will have in the end.

Because three days after they laid his battered body in a borrowed tomb Jesus burst forth again in living flesh, death has lost its sting for all believers. Your risen and ascended Lord makes you this promise: "I am the resurrection and the life. Whoever believes in me, though he die, yet shall he live, and everyone who lives and believes in me shall never die" (John 11:25–26).

The life Jesus gives you by his cross and resurrection is everlasting. Your sufferings, though they may linger on and on, are temporary by comparison. To know Christ and the power of his resurrection you must also share in the fellowship of his sufferings, which will come to an end one day soon.

With Jesus, it's already and not yet. Already now we have the reality of his forgiveness and consoling love. Yet the sufferings of this present time are not worth comparing to the glories that await us in the resurrection of the body and the life everlasting. Meanwhile we cast all our cares on him day by day, mingling our prayers and supplications with thanksgiving for his redeeming love.

If you live in fear or dread, if you're coping with loss or grief, if ever you contend with suffering or uncertainty, here's God's sure and certain promise, tailor-made for you:

> After you have suffered a little while,
> the God of all grace, who has called
> you to his eternal glory in Christ,
> will himself restore, confirm,
> strengthen, and establish you.
> To him be the dominion
> forever and ever.
> Amen.

(1 Peter 5:10–11)

Invitation to Prayer

Hear my prayer, O LORD;
let my cry come to you!

PSALM 102:1

Prayer for Any Time

This is a simple invitation to prayer for any time. When you offer your personal prayers, you might take a Bible verse or part of the Ten Commandments, the Apostles' Creed, or the Lord's Prayer and weave a prayer out of four cords: instruction, thanksgiving, confession of sin, and request.

Here's an example from Psalm 23: "The LORD is my shepherd; I shall not want" (Psalm 23:1 KJV). Instruction is straightforward: The Lord is my shepherd; he provides my every need. Thanksgiving could be something like: Thank you, Lord, for your tender care! A sin I might confess: Too often I trust in my own efforts and power, in money and possessions, making these idols over you. Finally a request: I need to rest securely in your protection.

Or all four parts might be woven together like this: Lord, you are my shepherd, who provides my every need. Thank you for your tender care—even when I don't see it or understand it! Too often I trust in my own efforts and power, in money and possessions, making these idols over you. Help me to rest securely in your protection. In the name of Jesus. Amen.

Prayer for Any Time

In the name of the Father and of the Son and of the Holy Spirit.
Amen.

Hear my cry, O God, *Psalm 61:1–3*
listen to my prayer;
from the end of the earth I call to you when my heart is faint.
Lead me to the rock that is higher than I,
for you have been my refuge, a strong tower against the enemy.

LORD, you know the deep places through which our lives must go: Help us, when we enter them, to lift our hearts to you; help us to be patient when we are afflicted, to be humble when we are in distress; and grant that the hope of your mercy may never fail us, and the consciousness of your loving kindness may never be clouded or hidden from our eyes; through Jesus Christ, your Son, our Lord.
Amen.

(Offer personal prayers. You might take a Bible verse and weave a prayer out of four cords: instruction, thanksgiving, confession of sin, and request.)

Our Father who art in heaven   *Matthew 6:9–13*
Hallowed be thy name;
thy kingdom come,
thy will be done on earth as it is in heaven.
Give us this day our daily bread;
and forgive us our trespasses as we forgive
    those who trespass against us;
and lead us not into temptation;
but deliver us from evil.
For thine is the kingdom and the power and
the glory forever and ever.

Let us bless the Lord.   *Psalm 103:1*
Thanks be to God.
The Lord bless us, defend us from all evil, and
bring us to everlasting life.
Amen.

Prayer for Morning

S ince the earliest days of the church, Christians have ordered their days with times of prayer at the beginning and end of each day.

Each line of these prayers was drawn from the Bible. In his inspired words the Holy Spirit intercedes for us in groanings too deep for words (Romans 8:26). God's words become our words, shaping and voicing our fears and faith.

In morning prayer believers consecrate their life and work to serve God and their neighbors. Use this ancient prayer to sanctify your life with God's word as you start each day. You can use it in a group setting—with the leader reading the plain text, and the group reading the words in bold. Or you can use it for your own private devotions.[8]

Prayer for Morning

The steadfast love of   *Lamentations 3:21–24*
the LORD never ceases;
his mercies never come to an end;
they are new every morning;
great is your faithfulness.
"The LORD is my portion," says my soul,
"therefore I will hope in him."

PSALMODY

O Lord, open my lips,   *Psalm 51:15*
and my mouth will declare your praise.
Make haste, O God, to deliver me!   *Psalm 70:1*
O LORD, make haste to help me!

I lift up my eyes to the hills.   *Psalm 121*
From where does my help come?
My help comes from the LORD,
who made heaven and earth.
He will not let your foot be moved;
he who keeps you will not slumber.
Behold, he who keeps Israel
will neither slumber nor sleep.
The LORD is your keeper;

the LORD is your shade on your right hand.
The sun shall not strike you by day,
nor the moon by night.
The LORD will keep you from all evil;
he will keep your life.
The LORD will keep your going out and
coming in
from this time forth forevermore.

**Glory be to the Father, and to the Son, and
to the Holy Spirit; as it was in the beginning,
is now, and will be forever. Amen.**

PRAYERS

Our Lord and Savior eagerly awaits our prayers:
"What father among you, if his son asks for a fish,
will instead of a fish give him a serpent; or if he
asks for an egg, will give him a scorpion? If you
then, who are evil, know how to give good gifts
to your children, how much more will the heavenly Father give the Holy Spirit to those who ask
him!" *Luke 11:11–13*
Thanks be to God.

Lord, hear my prayer; *Psalm 102:1*
and let my cry come to you.

Let us pray.

Almighty and everlasting God, you are always more ready to hear than we to pray, and to give more than we either desire or deserve: Pour upon us the abundance of your mercy, forgiving us those things of which our conscience is ashamed, and giving us those good things for which we are not worthy to ask, except through the merits and mediation of Jesus Christ our Savior; who lives and reigns with you and the Holy Spirit, one God, forever and ever. **Amen.**

(Offer personal prayers. You might take a Bible verse and weave a prayer out of four cords: instruction, thanksgiving, confession of sin, and request.)

Our Father who art in heaven   *Matthew 6:9–13*
Hallowed be thy name;
thy kingdom come,
thy will be done on earth as it is in heaven.
Give us this day our daily bread;
and forgive us our trespasses as we forgive
  those who trespass against us;
and lead us not into temptation;
but deliver us from evil.
For thine is the kingdom and the power and
the glory forever and ever.

Lord God, almighty and everlasting Father, you have brought us in safety to this new day: Preserve us with your mighty power, that we may not fall into sin, nor be overcome by adversity; and in all we do, direct us to the fulfilling of your purpose; through Jesus Christ our Lord.

Amen.

BENEDICTION

Now to him who is able to do far more abundantly than all that we ask or think, according to the power at work within us, to him be glory in the church and in Christ Jesus throughout all generations, forever and ever.

Amen. *Ephesians 3:20–21*

Let us bless the Lord. *Psalm 103:1*
Thanks be to God.

Prayer for Evening

S ince the earliest days of the church, Christians have ordered their days with times of prayer at the beginning and end of each day.

Each line of these prayers was drawn from the Bible. In his inspired words the Holy Spirit intercedes for us in groanings too deep for words (Romans 8:26). God's words become our words, shaping and voicing our fears and faith.

The order for evening prayer was called "Compline," referring to the day's completion, its end. Use this ancient prayer to sanctify your life with God's word as you prepare to rest in God's care. You can use it in a group setting—with the leader reading the plain text, and the group reading the words in bold. Or you can read it for your own private devotions.[9]

Prayer for Evening

The Lord Almighty grant us a peaceful night and a perfect end.

Amen.

Our help is in the Name of the Lord; *Psalm 124:8*
the maker of heaven and earth.

Confession

Let us confess our sins to God.

Silence may be kept.

Almighty God, our heavenly Father:
We have sinned against you,
through our own fault,
in thought, and word, and deed,
and in what we have left undone.
For the sake of your Son our Lord
Jesus Christ,
forgive us all our offenses;
and grant that we may serve you
in newness of life,
to the glory of your Name. Amen.

The Almighty God grant us forgiveness for all our sins, and the grace and comfort of the Holy Spirit.

Amen.

PSALMODY

Make haste, O God, to deliver me! *Psalm 70:1*
O LORD, make haste to help me!

Answer me when I call, *Psalm 4*
O God of my righteousness!
You have given me relief when I was in distress.
Be gracious to me and hear my prayer!
O men, how long shall my honor be turned
into shame?
**How long will you love vain words
and seek after lies?**
But know that the LORD has set apart the godly
for himself;
the LORD hears when I call to him.
Be angry, and do not sin;
**ponder in your own hearts on your beds,
and be silent.**
Offer right sacrifices
and put your trust in the LORD.

There are many who say,
"Who will show us some good?
**Lift up the light of your face upon us,
O Lord!"**
You have put more joy in my heart
**than they have when their grain and
wine abound.**
In peace I will both lie down and sleep;
**for you alone, O Lord, make me dwell
in safety.**

**Glory be to the Father, and to the Son, and
to the Holy Spirit; as it was in the beginning,
is now, and will be forever. Amen.**

Prayers

Our Lord Jesus invites us: "Come to me, all who
labor and are heavy-laden, and I will give you rest.
Take my yoke upon you, and learn from me; for
I am gentle and lowly in heart, and you will find
rest for your souls. For my yoke is easy, and my
burden is light." *Matthew 11:28–30*

Thanks be to God.

Into your hands, O Lord,   *Psalm 31:5*
I commit my spirit;
**for you have redeemed me, O Lord,
faithful God.**

Keep me, O Lord,   *Psalm 17:8*
as the apple of your eye;
hide me in the shadow of your wings.

Lord, hear my prayer;   *Psalm 102:1*
and let my cry come to you.

Let us pray.

Almighty and everlasting God, you are always more ready to hear than we to pray, and to give more than we either desire or deserve: Pour upon us the abundance of your mercy, forgiving us those things of which our conscience is ashamed, and giving us those good things for which we are not worthy to ask, except through the merits and mediation of Jesus Christ our Savior; who lives and reigns with you and the Holy Spirit, one God, forever and ever.
Amen.

(Offer personal prayers. You might take a Bible verse and weave a prayer out of four cords: instruction, thanksgiving, confession of sin, and request.)

Our Father who art in heaven *Matthew 6:9–13*
Hallowed be thy name;
thy kingdom come,
thy will be done on earth as it is in heaven.
Give us this day our daily bread;
and forgive us our trespasses as we forgive
those who trespass against us;
and lead us not into temptation;
but deliver us from evil.
For thine is the kingdom and the power and
the glory forever and ever.

Keep watch, dear Lord, with those who work, or watch, or weep this night, and give your angels charge over those who sleep. Tend the sick, Lord Christ; give rest to the weary, bless the dying, soothe the suffering, pity the afflicted, shield the joyous; and all for your love's sake.
Amen.

Guide us waking, O Lord, and guard us sleeping; that awake we may watch with Christ, and asleep we may rest in peace.

BENEDICTION

Let us bless the Lord.   *Psalm 103:1*

Thanks be to God.

The almighty and merciful Lord, Father, Son, and
Holy Spirit, bless us and keep us.

Amen.

"Jesus, Priceless Treasure"

JOHANN FRANCK

Jesus, priceless treasure,
Fount of purest pleasure,
Truest friend to me,
Ah, how long in anguish
Shall my spirit languish,
Yearning, Lord, for Thee?
Thou art mine, O Lamb divine!
I will suffer naught to hide Thee;
Naught I ask beside Thee.

In Thine arms I rest me;
Foes who would molest me
Cannot reach me here.
Though the earth be shaking,
Ev'ry heart be quaking,
Jesus calms my fear.
Lightnings flash and thunders crash;
Yet, though sin and hell assail me,
Jesus will not fail me.

Satan, I defy thee;
Death, I now decry thee;
Fear, I bid thee cease.
World, thou shalt not harm me
Nor thy threats alarm me
While I sing of peace.
God's great pow'r guards ev'ry hour;
Earth and all its depths adore Him,
Silent bow before Him.

Hence, all earthly treasure!
Jesus is my pleasure,
Jesus is my choice.
Hence, all empty glory!
Naught to me thy story
Told with tempting voice.
Pain or loss, or shame or cross,
Shall not from my Savior move me
Since He deigns to love me.

Evil world, I leave thee;
Thou canst not deceive me,
Thine appeal is vain.
Sin that once did blind me,
Get thee far behind me,
Come not forth again.
Past thy hour, O pride and pow'r;
Sinful life, thy bonds I sever,
Leave thee now forever.

Hence, all fear and sadness!
For the Lord of gladness,
Jesus, enters in.
Those who love the Father,
Though the storms may gather,
Still have peace within.
Yea, whate'er I here must bear,
Thou art still my purest pleasure,
Jesus, priceless treasure!

Notes

1. C. S. Lewis, *The Problem of Pain* (Macmillan, 1959), 81.

2. These are the words of the rite for individual confession in *Lutheran Service Book* (Concordia, 2006), 292. They accurately sum up my situation before God most days.

3. Thomas Kelly, "Stricken, Smitten, and Afflicted," *Lutheran Service Book*, no. 451, v. 2.

4. Here, I'm using the ESV's alternate translation.

5. The church has a long tradition of describing Jesus' death and resurrection this way. It's often called the "baited Leviathan" metaphor. It pulls together Hebrews 2:14–15 and Job 41:1.

6. Thomas Ken, "All Praise to Thee, My God, This Night," *Lutheran Service Book*, no. 883, v. 3.

7. The Rite of Committal, *Lutheran Service Book Pastoral Care Companion* (Concordia, 2007), 134.

8. "Prayer for Morning" is adapted from "Daily Morning Prayer: Rite Two," *The Book of Common Prayer* (Oxford University Press, 1979), 75–102. It also uses "Proper 22," *The Book of Common Prayer,* 234.

9. "Prayer for Evening" is adapted from "Compline," *The Book of Common Prayer*, 127–35. It also uses "Proper 22," *The Book of Common Prayer*, 234.

PASTORS CARE FOR A SOUL IN THE WAY A DOCTOR CARES FOR A BODY.

In a time when many churches have lost sight of the real purpose of the church, *The Care of Souls* invites a new generation of pastors to form the godly habits and practical wisdom needed to minister to the hearts and souls of those committed to their care.

"Pastoral theology at its best. Every pastor, and everyone who wants to be a pastor, should read this book."
—Timothy George, Founding Dean, Beeson Divinity School, Samford University; General Editor, Reformation Commentary on Scripture